STUDY GUIDE

Who is the Holy Spirit?

Sinclair Ferguson

LIGONIER MINISTRIES

Renew your Mind.

LIGONIER.ORG | 800-435-4343

1

Order from Chaos

MESSAGE INTRODUCTION

Many Christians have either heard, or even muttered, the phrase, "The Holy Spirit is the forgotten person of the Trinity." This assertion misses the real problem in the church today, a problem not extant in generations past. Christians know about the Holy Spirit, but, unlike the Father or the Son, they don't really know who the Holy Spirit is. In this lecture series, Dr. Sinclair Ferguson purposes to remove this ignorance by exploring the questions of the identity of the Spirit, the nature of His character, how we, as Christians, may come to know and have fellowship with Him, and more.

SCRIPTURE READINGS

Genesis 1:1–2, 26; 2:7; Exodus 31:1–11; Luke 1:8–17, 26–38; John 16:4–15; 1 Corinthians 6:19–20; 2 Corinthians 13:14; Revelation 22:17

LEARNING OBJECTIVES

1. To introduce the aims of the lecture series:
   a. What person is the Spirit?
   b. What kind of character does He have?
   c. How can we come to know Him and have fellowship with Him?
   d. How is it to our advantage that the Lord Jesus has gone away and that the Holy Spirit has come to the church?
2. To explain how the Spirit is the expression of the inner drive and desire of God
3. To illuminate the Spirit's role in the shaping and filling of creation
4. To demonstrate how the Spirit works in bringing man into fellowship with God

QUOTATION

Nevertheless, I tell you the truth: it is to your advantage that I go away, for if I do not go away, the Helper will not come to you. But if I go, I will send him to you.

—John 16:7

LECTURE OUTLINE

I. Who is the Holy Spirit?
   A. The etymology of the word "spirit"
      i.   The Hebrew word "ruah" and the Greek word "pneuma," which mean "spirit," are onomatopoetic.
      ii. Both these words describe the wind, or even a gale.
      iii. These words point to expressions of great effectiveness. In other words, they point to the driving energy or the characteristics of an individual as that individual expresses himself or herself to others in personal contact and personal communication.
   B. The revelation of God in the Holy Spirit
      i.   The Holy Spirit expresses the inner drive and desire of God in creation and in redemption and communicates God to us.
      ii. God reveals Himself in the Holy Spirit.
         1. He reveals Himself in an accommodating manner.
         2. He does so in order that His creation might have communion with Him.

II. The Presence of the Holy Spirit in Scripture
   A. All of Scripture reveals the Holy Spirit and His work in redemptive history.
   B. The very beginning of Scripture points to the Spirit's activity.
      i.   Genesis 1:2 describes the Holy Spirit as hovering over the original created mass.
         1. The original created mass is formless and empty.
         2. The Spirit hovers over the water in order that He might bring form and fullness to the formlessness and emptiness.
            a. The Spirit performs this same activity in salvation.
            b. The Spirit brings form and shape to formless lives dead in sin.
      ii. The Spirit brings shape and fullness to creation in order to make a temple, a meeting place, for God to meet with and have fellowship with His creation, particularly man.
         1. Psalm 19:1: the Spirit brings order and fullness in order that creation might receive the knowledge of God and worship Him.
         2. Genesis 1:27 and 2:7: These verses contain expressions of what God means to do through the power of the Spirit.
            a. God desires man to lead the worship of the Lord in His creation

b. The work of the Spirit, as recounted in numerous passages (e.g. Exodus 31:1–11; Luke 1:8–17, 26–38; John 16:4–15; 1 Corinthians 6:19–20; 2 Corinthians 13:14; Revelation 22:17), serves to lead God's people to a place where they may worship and glorify Him.

STUDY QUESTIONS

1. The Hebrew word "ruah" and the Greek word "pneuma," apart from meaning spirit, also mean _____ .
    a. wind
    b. fire
    c. water
    d. earth

2. God personally expresses Himself, His character, and His power to us through His Spirit.
    a. True
    b. False

3. God created everything simultaneously and the days of creation are pictures to help us understand the different elements of creation.
    a. True
    b. False

4. The Holy Spirit, by forming and filling the shapeless, empty mass, is creating a temple, a meeting place, for God to have fellowship with His creation.
    a. True
    b. False

5. The Spirit has brought order and fullness into the creation so that we might _____ .
    a. adore Him
    b. worship Him
    c. know Him
    d. all of the above

BIBLE STUDY AND DISCUSSION QUESTIONS

1. What does Dr. Ferguson mean when He describes the Spirit as God's inner drive and desire? What does this reveal about God's self-revelation?

2. Why must God accommodate His revelation to human beings? How does this fact demonstrate the mercy and grace of God?

3. Do you struggle to maintain a proper understanding of God in the fullness of His Trinitarian character, focusing instead on one Person of the Godhead at a time? Why do you think this occurs? How will you remedy this difficulty?

4. What role does the Spirit of God, described as hovering over the waters in Genesis 1:2, play in the creation account of Genesis? How does He interact with the formlessness and emptiness? How does this parallel salvation?

5. How does the Holy Spirit's work in the forming and filling of creation establish a meeting place between God and His creation, especially man? What places in Scripture point to this reality?

2

The Face of God

MESSAGE INTRODUCTION

Many people have claimed at various times and in various ways that the God of the Old Testament is not the same God as the God of the New Testament. Sadly, this assertion misunderstands the nature and purposes of God. God is immutable: He does not change in His nature, character, will, or purposes. Nonetheless, He has chosen to reveal His person and plans progressively in the history of redemption through His Spirit. This does not mean that the Spirit did not reveal the face of God at all in the Old Testament. On the contrary, the Old Testament reveals that the Spirit disclosed the very personal nature of our Lord to His people throughout the old covenant while pointing forward to the fullness of this disclosure in Jesus Christ.

SCRIPTURE READINGS

Genesis 1:2; 2:7; 41:38; Exodus 13:3–11, 30–35; Numbers 11:16–30; 2 Samuel 23:1–7; Psalm 51:9–12; 104:29–30; 139; Isaiah 63:9–10; Ezekiel 39:29; Daniel 1:17–21; 2:46–49; Matthew 11:28; Ephesians 4:30; 1 Peter 1:10–12; 2 Peter 1:21

LEARNING OBJECTIVES

1. To explore how the Holy Spirit worked in the old covenant, as recorded in the Old Testament, to prepare God's people for the coming of the Lord, Jesus Christ
2. To understand the personhood of the Spirit
3. To comprehend that the Spirit wants to bring God's people into an intimate relationship with the Lord
4. To see the progressive nature of the work of the Spirit

QUOTATION

> *Where shall I go from your Spirit?*
> *Or where shall I flee from your presence?*
> *If I ascend to heaven, you are there!*
> *If I make my bed in Sheol, you are there!*
> *If I take the wings of the morning*
> *and dwell in the uttermost parts of the sea,*
> *even there your hand shall lead me,*
> *and your right hand shall hold me.*
>
> —Psalm 139:7–10

LECTURE OUTLINE

I. The Spirit of God and the Face of God
    A. The Spirit of God makes Christians conscious of God's presence.
        i. Psalm 139: You cannot run from God in His creation.
        ii. Psalm 104:29–30: The Spirit of God is not only the expression of the presence of God, but the Spirit unveils the face of God for us.
            1. The Spirit reveals more than just God's attributes. He reveals the very face of God.
            2. The Old Testament reveals this in many places (e.g. Ezek. 39:29; Psalm 51).
    B. The Spirit reveals the face of God, the personal nature of the Lord, in many ways in the old covenant.
        i. The Spirit reveals God's personal love for His people by granting them wisdom.
            1. Genesis 41:38: God gives Joseph wisdom, as recognized by Pharaoh.
            2. Daniel 1:17–21; 2:46–49: Nebuchadnezzar acknowledges that God has given Daniel wisdom.
            3. The Spirit teaches God's people wisdom, as even non-believers attest.
        ii. The Spirit reveals God in His Word.
            1. The Holy Spirit instructs God's people by His Word throughout the old covenant.
            2. Prophets played a key role in this instruction.
        iii. The Spirit reveals God by giving His people gifts.
            1. The Spirit gives gifts for the building of the tabernacle (Ex. 31)
            2. The tabernacle served as a place in which the people met with God.
        iv. The Spirit reveals God by leading His people into freedom and a personal relationship with the Lord.
            1. Isaiah 63:10 and Ephesians 4:30 commmand God's people not to grieve the Holy Spirit. This demonstrates His personhood.
            2. This language, seen in the context of the exodus, reveals that the Spirit's role in the exodus was to lead God's people into freedom so that they might have a personal relationship with Him.

II. The Progressive Work of the Spirit
  A. The Spirit points forward to the fullness of the new covenant.
     i. Not all of God's people in the old covenant received the fullness of His revelation.
        1. Numbers 11:16–30: The Spirit is distributed from Moses into just the elders.
        2. Moses declares that the Spirit was upon all of God's people.
     ii. Prophets received a greater revelation of the Spirit.
        1. The Spirit worked in them in order to reveal His Word to the people.
        2. As believers in the new covenant, we all have the fullness of the Spirit and immediate access to our Savior, Jesus Christ.
  B. The ultimate goal of the Spirit's work is to bring God's people into rest.
     i. The fall in the garden of Eden stripped man of rest.
     ii. The Holy Spirit points God's believers in the old covenant to the final rest in Jesus Christ (Matt. 11:28).

STUDY QUESTIONS

1. The Spirit of God unveils the attributes of God, but not His person.
   a. True
   b. False

2. The kings and lords of foreign lands recognized the Spirit of the Lord in Joseph, Daniel, and other because they possessed _____ .
   a. good looks
   b. excellent rhetoric
   c. wisdom
   d. intelligence

3. When the prophets speak about the hand of the Lord being upon them, they mean that the Spirit of the Lord has _____ .
   a. disciplined them
   b. spoken to them
   c. touched them physically
   d. come upon them

4. All of God's people experienced the fullness of His revelation through the Spirit in the old covenant.
   a. True
   b. False

5. All old covenant believers could aspire to be prophets of the Lord.
   a. True
   b. False

BIBLE STUDY AND DISCUSSION QUESTIONS

1. How does the Holy Spirit unveil the face of God? What does it mean, "to unveil the face of God"? What does this reveal about God's attributes?

2. How does the Holy Spirit reveal the Father in the wisdom He grants to His people? Explain your answer in light of the biblical accounts of Joseph and Daniel. Can you describe any events in your own life in which the wisdom of God in you has instigated notice and remark by unbelievers?

3. How does the Holy Spirit instruct God's people? Support your answer from Scripture.

4. What do Isaiah 63:9–10 and Ephesians 4:30 reveal to us about the nature of the Holy Spirit? How is this demonstrated in the work of the Exodus?

5. Is there a progress to the work of the Spirit? If so, why? If there is progress to the work of the Spirit, to what goal does it point?

3

The Spirit of the Lord

MESSAGE INTRODUCTION

It is tempting to understand the Spirit as an impersonal force fulfilling the purposes of God mechanically. However, the Scriptures paint a different picture, and they portray the Spirit as anything but impersonal. The third person of the Trinity is personal, and His role in the life and ministry of Jesus attests to this fact. The Spirit is the lifelong companion and friend of Jesus, and the two were never, nor ever will be, apart. This revelation is marvelous, and our wonder should increase as we consider Jesus' role in sending His Spirit, His companion and friend, to dwell with us.

SCRIPTURE READINGS

Genesis 1:2; Isaiah 11:2–3; 42; 49; 52–53; 61:1–2; Psalm 27; Matthew 5–7; Luke 1:26–38; 2:41–52; 4:17–21; John 14:8–11, 15–17; 1 Peter 1:10–12

LEARNING OBJECTIVES

1. To understand how Jesus reveals the Father and the Spirit
2. To see the close relationship between Jesus and the Holy Spirit
3. To comprehend the role of the Spirit in Jesus' conception, infancy, and childhood

QUOTATION

Now all the furniture is in the room, but it's only when you turn the light on that you realize all the furniture is there. This is very much like the Old Testament revelation of God. The God of the Old Testament is the same as the God of the New Testament. He is Father and Son and Holy Spirit, but there's a sense in which, for believers under the old covenant, they lived in a kind of darkened room.

—B.B. Warfield

LECTURE OUTLINE

I. Jesus Christ's Revelation

    A. Scripture proclaims that Jesus reveals the Father.

    B. Similar to His revelation of the Father, Jesus reveals the Holy Spirit as well.

        i. John 14:17: "You [the disciples] know him [the Spirit], because he dwells with you and will be in you."

            1. Jesus does not refer here to a difference between old covenant and new covenant believers.

            2. The Spirit has been with the disciples because the Lord Jesus has been with them.

        ii. Just as the disciples know the Father because of Jesus' fellowship with Him, the disciples know the Spirit because of His fellowship with Jesus.

II. The Fellowship of Jesus and the Spirit

    A. The prophet Isaiah illustrates the relation of the Spirit to Jesus' ministry more than any other.

        i. Isaiah 42, 49, 50, and 52–53 point to the presence of the Spirit with the Lord's Suffering Servant, Jesus.

        ii. Isaiah 61: this chapter reveals that the Holy Spirit is the lifelong companion, supporter, encourager, counselor, and director of the Lord Jesus Christ.

    B. The Spirit plays an important role in the infancy and childhood of Jesus.

        i. Luke 1:26–38: These verses demonstrate the Spirit's important role in the conception of the Savior of the world.

            1. v.35: The Holy Spirit will come upon Mary and overshadow her.

                a. Similar to Genesis 1:2, the Spirit gives form and life to Jesus inside the virgin Mary.

                b. The Holy Spirit is present and ministering to Jesus from His embryonic state.

            2. Out of the virgin's barrenness, the Holy Spirit brings life to the one who will lead His people out of bondage.

        ii. Luke 2:41–52: The Spirit ministers to Jesus in His childhood.

            1. Jesus' parents don't know His whereabouts and frantically search for Him in Jerusalem.

            2. Upon finding Him, Jesus responds to Mary's interrogation by saying, "Why were you looking for me? Did you not know that I must be in my Father's house?"

                a. Jesus, filled with the Spirit, knew where to find His Father.

                b. His parents should have known that their son would seek out this opportunity to meet with His heavenly Father.

            3. Jesus increased in wisdom and stature because He was walking step by step in fellowship with the Holy Spirit, who was giving Him wisdom.

STUDY QUESTIONS

1. Jesus reveals the Father.
   a. True
   b. False

2. When Jesus said, "You know him [the Spirit], for he dwells with you and will be with you," He meant that _____ .
   a. Old Testament and New Testament believers were different
   b. the disciples knew the Spirit because He had been with them in Jesus
   c. each disciple had the fullness of the indwelling of the Spirit
   d. the disciples were perfect

3. The prophet who makes clearest to us the ministry of the Holy Spirit in relation to the Lord Jesus is _____ .
   a. Isaiah
   b. Jeremiah
   c. Amos
   d. Malachi

4. The Spirit is the lifelong companion, supporter, encourager, counselor, and director of the Lord Jesus Christ.
   a. True
   b. False

5. The Holy Spirit became Jesus' companion and friend at the beginning of His ministry.
   a. True
   b. False

BIBLE STUDY AND DISCUSSION QUESTIONS

1. How does Jesus reveal the Father? How does Jesus reveal the Holy Spirit? Are there differences in these revelations? Why or why not?

2. Read the passages in Isaiah referenced above in the section "Scripture Readings." What do these passages disclose about Jesus Christ and His relationship to the Spirit?

3. What was the role of the Holy Spirit in the infancy of Jesus? How does Genesis 1:2 illuminate the work of the Spirit in Luke 1 and the conception of Jesus?

4. What did Jesus mean when he said to Mary, "Why were you looking for me? Did you not know that I must be in my Father's house?" How did Jesus "grow in wisdom and stature"?

5. Did Jesus know His messianic role as a young boy, even His eventual death on the cross? How would Jesus have arrived at this knowledge?

WOMEN'S BIBLE STUDY!

Faith Evangelical Presbyterian Church

Thursday, January 13, 2022
10:00 AM
Fellowship Hall
12-week Video Bible Study led by Beth Rosenbush
Childcare Provided
Books $11/Scholarships Available

FAITH CHURCH
MAGNIFY | MANIFEST | MULTIPLY

4

Dwelling Within

MESSAGE INTRODUCTION

The temptations endured by Jesus in the wilderness are remarkable accounts of Jesus' righteous fortitude in the face of the most trying conditions. Having received the approval of the Father and the anointing of the Spirit at His baptism, Jesus, debilitated and suffering, succeeded where our forefather, the first Adam, failed, setting the stage for a ministry that would lead to His victory in the resurrection. However, Jesus did not undergo these trials alone, but He received the ministrations and support of His companion, the Holy Spirit, the same person who led Jesus into the wilderness. The Spirit orchestrated these events and assisted Jesus in order that He might rebuke the Devil and move into His rightful position as our Savior.

SCRIPTURE READINGS

Genesis 1:2; 8:6–19; Deuteronomy 29:29; Matthew 3:13–17; Mark 1:9–11; Luke 3:21–22, 23–38; 4:1–13; John 1:29–34; 2 Corinthians 5:17; 13:14

LEARNING OBJECTIVES

1. To receive a stronger grasp of our limitation in understanding the interrelationship of the persons of the Trinity
2. To comprehend the significance behind Jesus' baptism and temptations in the wilderness
3. To understand the role of the Spirit in Jesus' baptism and temptations in the wilderness

QUOTATION

The secret things belong to the LORD our God, but the things that are revealed belong to us and to our children forever, that we may do all the words of this law.

—Deuteronomy 29:29

LECTURE OUTLINE

I. The Mystery of the Trinity

    A. Deuteronomy 29:29: There are many things about the Trinity that we wouldn't be able to understand if God told them to us.

    B. God has chosen not to disclose other aspects about the Trinity.

    C. Yet, despite the previous facts, God does disclose information about the inter-relation of the Trinity in His Word, and Jesus provides the access to knowing the Father and the Spirit.

II. The Revelation of the Holy Spirit in the Baptism and Temptations of Jesus

    A. At Jesus' baptism, the Holy Spirit descends upon Jesus in the form of a dove.

        i. There is an analogy between the appearance of a dove and Genesis 1:2

            1. The Holy Spirit, in His power, begins a new creation at Jesus' baptism, similar to His creative work as recorded in Genesis 1.

            2. Luke's placement of Jesus' genealogy after the baptism testifies to His creative power that goes all the way back to the beginning of creation.

            3. 2 Corinthians 5:17: "If we are in Christ, we have entered into a new creation."

        ii. The appearance of the dove hearkens back to the account of Noah in Genesis 8:6–19.

            1. Noah could not provide the rest promised by his name.

            2. Jesus' baptism demonstrates that He will receive the deluge of God's judgment in His true and final baptism on the cross.

        iii. The location of Jesus' baptism at the Jordan also possesses significance.

            1. The Israelites crossed the Jordan on dry ground into the Promised Land with the ark of the covenant.

            2. Jesus will lead His people into the eternal rest of the Promised Land.

    B. The anointing of Jesus

        i. The Holy Spirit anoints Jesus to fulfill the offices of prophet, priest, and king

            1. Prophet = to deliver God's message

            2. Priest = to offer Himself on the cross

            3. King = to reign over His people and the whole earth

        ii. This anointing signifies Jesus entering into a different, dynamic stage of redemptive history.

    C. The temptation of Jesus

        i. The Holy Spirit "throws" Jesus into the wilderness in order that the Devil might tempt Him.

            1. The temptation of Jesus parallels the temptation of Adam.

               a. While Adam endured temptation in comfort, fullness, and peace, Jesus endured temptation in harshness, want, and hostility. (Note Mark's statement about the wild beasts surrounding Jesus.)

b. While Adam failed the single temptation of the Devil, Jesus re-buffed His three attempts and sent him fleeing.

2. The Holy Spirit leads Jesus into the wilderness so that He might empower Him to overcome the wiles of the Devil and move into the role of the second Adam.

ii. The same Spirit who overcame the Devil in Jesus resides in God's peo-ple today, who serve as prophets, priests, and kings by virtue of Jesus death, resurrection, ascension, and His sending of the Spirit.

STUDY QUESTIONS

1. Christians should not glorify the Spirit.
   a. True
   b. False

2. God has revealed to Christians in His Word the entire interrelationship of the Father, Son, and Holy Spirit.
   a. True
   b. False

3. Modalism/Sabellianism asserts that the Father, Son, and Holy Spirit are

   _____ .

   a. different modes/aspects
   b. distinct persons
   c. distinct beings
   d. different substances

4. The Holy Spirit descended upon Jesus at His baptism in the form of a

   _____ .

   a. raven
   b. eagle
   c. wood pigeon
   d. dove

5. Jesus is anointed at His baptism as a prophet and priest only.
   a. True
   b. False

BIBLE STUDY AND DISCUSSION QUESTIONS

1. Why is man unable to know everything about the interrelationship of the Father, Son, and Holy Spirit? What information does God's Word reveal about this inter-relationship? Provide Scripture references.

2. How were the three persons of the Trinity in fellowship with one another at Jesus' baptism? Why does Luke place the genealogy of Jesus immediately after Jesus' baptism?

3. Why does the Spirit take the form of a dove at Jesus' baptism? What connection does this have with Noah? Is there any significance in the fact that Jesus' baptism took place in the Jordan River?

4. What is the significance behind Jesus' anointing at His baptism? How is the baptism of Jesus different from our baptism?

5. Why did the Holy Spirit drive Jesus into the wilderness? What comparisons is Scripture making between Adam and Jesus? What role does the Holy Spirit play in this episode? What does this mean for Christians today?

5

Trinitarian Fellowship

MESSAGE INTRODUCTION

Companionship plays a large role in the life of Christians and non-Christians alike. It is wonderful to possess friends and loved ones with whom you can reveal the inner workings of your heart without fear, rejection, and spite. We don't need to explain ourselves or our emotions to these loved ones. They know us just as we know them. The Father, Son, and Spirit experience this mutual love, openness, and adoration in a manner that cannot be explained or replicated. When Jesus rejoiced in the Spirit, He marveled at the work of His companion, the Holy Spirit, who sought to bring about the purposes of the Father so that the Savior, who He had nurtured and preserved throughout His entire life, might achieve the joy the Father had intended for Him since the beginning of time.

SCRIPTURE READINGS

Isaiah 61:1–2; Luke 4:14–15, 17–21; 10:21–24; 11:14–23; 12:10; John 10:14–18; 14:15–17

LEARNING OBJECTIVES

1. To understand the role of the Spirit in Jesus' life and ministry
2. To comprehend what it means when Scripture describes Jesus as "rejoicing in the Spirit"
3. To see the heinousness of blaspheming the Holy Spirit
4. To appreciate the intimacy of the Spirit with the Son

QUOTATION

In that same hour he rejoiced in the Holy Spirit and said, "I thank you, Father, Lord of heaven and earth, that you have hidden these things from the wise and understanding and revealed them to little children; yes, Father, for such was your gracious will. All things have been handed over to me by my Father, and no one knows who the Son is except the Father, or who the Father is except the Son and anyone to whom the Son chooses to reveal him."

—Luke 10:21–22

LECTURE OUTLINE

I. The Role of the Holy Spirit in the Life and Ministry of Jesus
   A. The Holy Spirit enabled Jesus to loose His people from the bondage of sin.
      i. Luke 4:17–21: Jesus read from Isaiah 61:1–2 at the synagogue in Nazareth.
      ii. The Spirit's anointing of Jesus allowed Him to say to the people that He had come to take away their sin and liberate them from their depravity.
   B. The Spirit enabled Jesus to bring restoration during His ministry in a manner never before seen in redemptive history.
      i. Jesus healed many and brought restoration to a sick and hurting land.
      ii. Jesus did not heal everyone, but He brought healing and restoration in order to provide a glimpse of the future, permanent restoration.
   C. The Spirit enabled Jesus to deliver the oppressed from demonic bondage.
      i. The ministry of Jesus witnessed the largest influx of demonic activity in the history of the world.
         1. Demonic forces understood their time of preeminence was drawing to a close.
         2. Their master had been thwarted by Jesus and they sought to strike at Him in a last-ditch effort to prevent His salvific work.
      ii. The Holy Spirit empowered Jesus to establish His kingdom and defeat His demonic opponents.

II. Jesus Rejoiced in the Holy Spirit
   A. Luke 10:21–24 displays the special communion Jesus has with the Holy Spirit.
      i. Jesus rejoiced in the Spirit upon hearing about the works of His disciples.
         1. Jesus marvels at the Spirit's activity in His disciples for the kingdom.
         2. In ecstatic joy, Jesus thanks His Father for the communion He has with Him and the Spirit.
      ii. The Spirit worked in the disciples to enhance and further Jesus' kingdom.
   B. Jesus proclaims that blaspheming the Holy Spirit is an unforgivable sin (Luke 12:10).

i.   When Jesus refers to blaspheming the Holy Spirit, He means resisting the ministry of the Spirit.

ii. When one resists the Spirit, he resists the will of the Father. Resistance to the will of the Spirit strikes at the joy of Jesus, which is the foremost goal of the Father.

1.   The Spirit worked in the life of Jesus to increase His wisdom and stature, which in turn increased the Father's favor toward Him.

2.   Jesus stated that the Father loved Him because of His willingness to lay down His life for His sheep (John 10:14–17). In a human way of speaking, Jesus found the utmost favor of His Father in this act, for which the Spirit prepared and fortified Him.

STUDY QUESTIONS

1. All inhabitants of Nazareth accepted Jesus' declaration that He was the Spirit-filled Messiah prophesied by Isaiah.
    a. True
    b. False

2. The Bible contains a vast number of accounts chronicling demonic activity and demonic possessions.
    a. True
    b. False

3. Jesus rejoiced in the Spirit when He heard the disciples recounting their exploits (as recorded in Luke 10) because He marveled at the Spirit's activity.
    a. True
    b. False

4. Jesus declares the unforgivable sin to be _____ .
    a. dishonoring father or mother
    b. blaspheming the Holy Spirit
    c. blaspheming the Son of God
    d. murder

5. The Father's love for Jesus was never greater than at Jesus' _____ .
    a. baptism
    b. crucifixion
    c. birth
    d. circumcision

BIBLE STUDY AND DISCUSSION QUESTIONS

1. Why did Jesus choose Isaiah 61:1–2 to read at the synagogue in Nazareth? What does this passage say about the role of the Holy Spirit in the life and ministry of Jesus?

2. Why did Jesus perform miracles? What do the miracles signify, and what insight do they give us about the future?

3. Why is there such a concentration of demons in Israel during the time of Jesus' ministry? What role does the Holy Spirit play in Jesus activity?

4. What does it mean when Scripture states that Jesus "rejoiced in the Spirit"?

5. Why does Jesus proclaim blaspheming the Holy Spirit to be an unforgivable sin? Why is it so heinous?

6

The Sustainer

MESSAGE INTRODUCTION

The picture of Jesus on the cross at Calvary is the loneliest portrait of a man in the history of the world. He hung dying, incurring the wrath of His Father as He bore the sins of the world. These sins were not His own, and He had never before been prevented from communing with His heavenly Father. Yet, the Holy Spirit sustained Jesus through His sacrifice, and He preserved Him just as He had done from the moment of Christ's conception. This same Spirit who fortified Jesus to atone for the sins of His people dwells in us today, an unspeakable privilege that should unite the church in humility, thankfulness, and love.

SCRIPTURE READINGS

Psalm 22; 24; Matthew 27:46; John 14:15–17; Acts 1:9; Romans 1:4; 1 Corinthians 15:42–49; 2 Corinthians 3:16–18; Hebrews 9:11–14

LEARNING OBJECTIVES

1. To see how the Holy Spirit remained with Jesus at the end of His ministry and life
2. To understand the complete harmony in which Jesus and the Spirit commune
3. To recognize that marriage serves as a hint of the relationship between the persons of the Trinity, particularly the Son and the Spirit
4. To realize that the same Spirit that dwells in Jesus dwells in each of His sheep

QUOTATION

For if the blood of goats and bulls, and the sprinkling of defiled persons with the ashes of a heifer, sanctify for the purification of the flesh, how much more will the blood of Christ, who through the eternal Spirit offered himself without blemish to God, purify our conscience from dead works to serve the living God.

—Hebrews 9:13–14

LECTURE OUTLINE

I.   The Role of the Holy Spirit at the End of Jesus' Life

   A. Hebrews 9:14: As Jesus offered Himself as the atoning sacrifice on the cross, the Holy Spirit sustained Him.

      i.   Jesus felt the abandonment of the Father as He bore the judgment of God's wrath upon sin.

      ii. The Holy Spirit sustained Jesus on the cross and enabled Him to bear the sins of the world.

   B. The Holy Spirit vindicated Jesus through His transforming power in the resurrection (Rom. 1:4).

   C. The Holy Spirit played an important role in the ascension of Jesus (Acts 1:9)

      i.   A cloud takes the ascending Jesus out of sight.

         1. This is the glory cloud revealed among the people of God during the old covenant.

         2. The Spirit ushers the victorious Jesus into the heavenly realm and the right hand of the Father.

      ii. The Spirit plays a role in Jesus life from His birth, to His ascension, and beyond.

   D. 1 Corinthians 15:42–49 and 2 Corinthians 3:16–18 speak about the nature of resurrection bodies.

      i.   Jesus body was sown in dishonor but raised in glory. Christians experience this same fate by their union with Jesus.

      ii. Paul explains that this knowledge only comes when the Spirit removes the veil of unbelief.

II. The Harmony of Jesus and the Spirit

   A. God has placed hints of his Trinitarian interrelation in His creation.

      i.   Marriage between man and a woman serves as one of these hints.

         1. As marriage partners progress, they learn more and more about each others' subtleties.

         2. They arrive at a place in which they can communicate without words because they know each other intimately.

      ii. The Holy Spirit and Jesus possess a harmony and intimacy far beyond a human marriage.

   B. Jesus sent His own Spirit to dwell in His people.

      i.   The same Spirit that dwells in Jesus dwells in believers.

      ii. This reality should cause believers to love and cherish one another naturally and humbly.

STUDY QUESTIONS

1. The Holy Spirit abandoned Jesus on the cross.
   a. True
   b. False

2. The clouds at Jesus' ascension signified the presence of _____ .
   a. a storm
   b. the Father
   c. the Holy Spirit
   d. God's wrath

3. Marriage is a hint from God about what His Trinitarian fellowship is like.
   a. True
   b. False

4. A different Spirit dwells in Jesus than the one that dwells in Christians.
   a. True
   b. False

5. In regards to the Spirit, we should focus our attention on the following question:_____
   a. "what does the Spirit mean to me?"
   b. "what does the Spirit mean to Jesus?"
   c. "what does the Spirit mean to the church?"
   d. "what does the Spirit mean to my spouse?"

BIBLE STUDY AND DISCUSSION QUESTIONS

1. Did the Holy Spirit abandon Jesus while He hung on the cross? If not, what role did the Spirit play in that act of atonement? In His resurrection?

2. Why does the book of Acts specifically mention the presence of clouds in the ascension of Jesus? What role does the Holy Spirit play in this episode in redemptive history? How did the early church understand this act?

3. Read 1 Corinthians 15:42–49 and 2 Corinthians 3:16–18. What is Paul saying in these passages about the relationship between Jesus and the Holy Spirit?

4. How does marriage reveal, in a truncated, imperfect manner, the interrelations of the persons of the Trinity, particularly the Son and the Spirit?

5. Since the same Spirit that dwells in Christ dwells in each one of His sheep, how should that affect the way Christians treat one another?

7

Rivers of Living Water

MESSAGE INTRODUCTION

New covenant believers receive such a fullness of the Spirit that sometimes we struggle to understand the conditions of believers in the old covenant. The Spirit withheld the fullness of His manifestation, and only some experienced a heightened revelation of His goodness. While this was more than sufficient for faith and worship, new covenant believers enjoy the astounding privilege of seeing the almighty God in the face of Jesus Christ. Jesus promised this blessing, and He fulfilled His promise at Pentecost, the unique event at which He poured out His Spirit in rivers of living water to His church.

SCRIPTURE READINGS

Genesis 1:2; Psalm 2; Isaiah 12:3; Joel 2:28–29; Zechariah 13:1; Luke 3:16; John 1:29–34; 7:37–39; 14:15–17; 16:8–11; Acts 1:1–11; 2:1–41

LEARNING OBJECTIVES

1. To understand the way in which Jesus gives His Spirit to His disciples
2. To comprehend the importance behind Jesus' words at the Feast of Booths as recounted in John 7
3. To understand the activity of the Spirit through Jesus at Pentecost

QUOTATION

If anyone thirsts, let him come to me and drink. Whoever believes in me, as the scriptures have said, out of his heart will flow rivers of living water.

—John 7:37–38

LECTURE OUTLINE

I. Rivers of Living Waters

    A. John 7:37–39: Jesus stood on the last day of the Feast of Booths and declared that the one who believed in Him, "out of his heart will flow rivers of living water."

        i. Jesus said this about the Spirit, who had not been given to the church.

        ii. Jesus, although generally reserved in His public disclosure, stood among the Jews and called for belief in Him.

            1. The ceremony of the Feast of Booths called for the pouring of water around the base of the altar of burnt offering while the Jews walked around it.

            2. The ceremony, although not prescribed in Scripture, served as a reminder of God's activity among His people and signified a longing for the outpouring of God's Spirit (Isa. 12:3).

    B. There are two different ways to translate Jesus' declaration.

        i. First option: out of the believer will flow rivers of living water.

        ii. Second option: Jesus refers to Himself as the rivers of living water.

        iii. Dr. Ferguson prefers the second option.

            1. Jesus will send the Spirit at Pentecost, and this will serve as the outpouring of the rivers of living water.

            2. The water that flowed from Jesus side when it was pierced also foreshadows this event.

II. Pentecost

    A. John the Baptist prophesied that Jesus would baptize with the Spirit and fire (Luke 3:16).

        i. The disciples obeyed Jesus' command and waited in Jerusalem for Jesus' Spirit.

        ii. Jesus sent His Spirit to the disciples on Pentecost in transforming, creative power.

    B. The Spirit worked in a unique manner on the day of Pentecost.

        i. Acts 2:2: The Holy Spirit came upon the disciples like a gale, echoing the creative power of Genesis 1:2.

        ii. The Holy Spirit rectified the dilemma fashioned at the Tower of Babel (Gen 11).

            1. Mankind sought to overthrow the rule of God, so God muddled their communication and scattered them across the earth.

            2. The Holy Spirit brings new community to what was formerly divided.

        iii. The list of nations provided by Luke in Acts demonstrates that the Holy Spirit was blessing all the nations through the seed of Abraham (Jesus).

        iv. The Holy Spirit fulfills the prophecy of Joel 2 and provides access to God through Jesus Christ to every Christian.

        v. As the messianic King prophesied in Psalm 2, the Holy Spirit brings all nations before Jesus to bow in homage to Him.

STUDY QUESTIONS

1. The fulfillment of Jesus' words in John 16:8–11 occurred at _____ .
   a. Passover
   b. the Feast of Booths
   c. Pentecost
   d. Christmas

2. When John records in the seventh chapter of His gospel that "the Spirit was not," He meant that the Spirit _____ .
   a. did not exist
   b. was displeased
   c. had not been given to the church
   d. resided in heaven only

3. The water that flowed from Jesus' pierced side after His death represents the life-giving Spirit He would send at Pentecost.
   a. True
   b. False

4. The Tower of Babel was an attempt by men to get closer to God so that they might worship Him better.
   a. True
   b. False

5. Pentecost is a fulfillment of God's promise that all the nations will be blessed by the seed of Abraham.
   a. True
   b. False

BIBLE STUDY AND DISCUSSION QUESTIONS

1. Why did Jesus stand among the people during the Feast of Booths and proclaim, "If anyone thirsts, let him come to me and drink. Whoever believes in me, as the scriptures have said, out of his heart will flow rivers of living water"? What significance did this carry in relation to the rites of the feast?

2. What are the interpretive difficulties surrounding Jesus' proclamation, "If anyone thirsts, let him come to me and drink. Whoever believes in me, as the scriptures have said, out of his heart will flow rivers of living water"? How does Dr. Ferguson resolve this issue? What is the significance of water and blood that flowed from Jesus' side after His death on the cross?

3. Is the outpouring of the Spirit that occurred at Pentecost repeated? Why or why not?

4. Why did the disciples of Jesus receive the ability to speak different languages? How does this relate to the Tower of Babel (Gen. 11)?

5. Read Joel 2:28–29. How is this prophecy fulfilled at Pentecost?

8

A Heavenly Birth

MESSAGE INTRODUCTION

For those who stand outside of faith, the message of the gospel may appear burdensome and shackling. Yet, this could not be farther from the truth. The regeneration of the Spirit liberates believers to turn their affections to Christ and put their faith in Him. God's people were created to enjoy this knowledge and love of the Savior, and they receive fulfillment only when their hearts are turned to Him. Jesus' yoke is easy and His burden is light (Matt. 11:30), and man remains in darkness, empty, burdened, and miserable, until the Spirit breathes life and light into his dead, sinful heart.

SCRIPTURE READINGS

John 1:12, 29–34; 3:1–21; 16:8–11; 1 Corinthians 12:13; Colossians 2:6–3:4; 1 Peter 1:23; James 1:18

LEARNING OBJECTIVES

1. To understand how the Holy Spirit works in the lives of individual believers
2. To comprehend how the Holy Spirit brings individuals into the kingdom of God

QUOTATION

Jesus answered, "Truly, truly, I say to you, unless one is born of water and the Spirit, he cannot enter the kingdom of God. That which is born of the flesh is flesh, and that which is born of the Spirit is spirit. Do not marvel that I said to you, 'You must be born again.' The wind blows where it wishes, and you hear its sound, but you do not know where it comes from or where it goes. So it is with everyone who is born of the Spirit."

—John 3:5–8

LECTURE OUTLINE

I. Our Participation with Jesus Christ

    A. Jesus performs many non-repeatable activities as the unique God-man and Messiah.

    B. Nonetheless, the Scriptures speak about Christians participating in these activities with Jesus (Col. 2:6–3:4).

       i. On the day of Pentecost, Jesus provides the great, once-and-for-all baptism of the Spirit.

      ii. Yet, as Paul states in 2 Corinthians 12:13, all Christians receive the baptism of the Holy Spirit, even if only later in time they are added to this outpouring.

II. The Role of the Holy Spirit in Regeneration

    A. John 3 provides a marvelous description by Jesus of the work of the Holy Spirit in regeneration.

       i. Nicodemus, "the teacher of Israel," comes to Jesus by night to speak to Him.

          1. Jesus claims that Nicodemus did not understand the necessity of the Spirit's regeneration for faith.

          2. Jesus' statement demonstrates that religious leaders may be considered great teachers in the church but not possess saving faith.

      ii. Jesus tells Nicodemus He must be "born again."

          1. Jesus means that Nicodemus must be born from above, or born again through the work of the Holy Spirit.

          2. This heavenly birth can only occur under the transforming power of the Spirit.

          3. Jesus uses the illustration of the wind blowing to clarify His point.

             a. No earthly resource can accomplish this.

             b. Only the Spirit, the *pneuma*, the wind, who possesses heavenly resources, can achieve this.

      iii. Jesus teaches that the bestowal of salvation rests in the hands of God alone.

          1. Like the wind, mankind cannot effect salvation.

          2. Salvation originates from the sovereign choice of God alone, and like the wind, you cannot know when or how the Spirit will regenerate someone.

      iv. Like the wind, the work of the Spirit produces effects in those who believe.

          1. Those who have been born into the kingdom of God by the work of the Spirit have the ability to see that Jesus is king in His kingdom.

          2. Regeneration brings light to darkened minds.

       v.   Regeneration brings liberation from bondage to sin.
          1.   No one can loose their shackles of bondage and will themselves into Jesus' kingdom.
          2.   Jesus' Spirit must liberate an individual's soul.
          3.   After the Spirit liberates an individual's soul, he is washed clean with the water of the Spirit and His affections turn toward Jesus.

B.   The Spirit regenerates, illuminates, liberates, and turns the affections of God's people to Jesus, after which they are able to follow the call of John 3:16: to believe in Jesus and have everlasting life.

STUDY QUESTIONS

1. In a real way, Christians participate in the once-for-all events of Jesus Christ's life (e.g. the crucifixion).
   a. True
   b. False

2. The Pharisee who met Jesus at night as recorded in John 3 was named

   _____ .

   a. Ehud
   b. Zechariah
   c. Simeon
   d. Nicodemus

3. Jesus imagery of wind in the bestowal of salvation demonstrates the _____ of God in this process.
   a. sovereignty
   b. goodness
   c. wrath
   d. wisdom

4. Regeneration, the new birth, illuminates darkened minds.
   a. True
   b. False

5. You know you have been born again if you believe in Jesus Christ as your Lord and Savior.
   a. True
   b. False

BIBLE STUDY AND DISCUSSION QUESTIONS

1. How do Christians in all ages relate to Pentecost? Does this diminish the uniqueness of the event? Why or why not?

2. Can an individual not be a believer and still know much about Christianity and do many things for the good of the church? Why or why not? Use Scripture to defend your position.

3. What does it mean to be "born from above"? What role does the Spirit play in this?

4. What significance does Jesus' likening salvation to the movement of wind hold? What does this say about the Spirit's role in salvation?

5. How does the Spirit free sinners from a state of bondage? Does this liberation free sinners from all forms of bondage? Why or why not?

9

A Heavenly Helper

MESSAGE INTRODUCTION

The thought of walking, sitting, and eating with Jesus brings Christians great joy, and His physical absence leaves us longing to be in His presence. As wonderful as this thought and longing is, we should not neglect the truth that Jesus has sent another helper. The Holy Spirit, the comforter, teacher, advocate, and homemaker, dwells within God's people and illuminates their hearts with the fullness of Christ. We see Christ clearly now because His companion, His Spirit, resides within us.

SCRIPTURE READINGS

John 3:1–21; 13:12; 14:15–31; 15:26–27

LEARNING OBJECTIVES

1. To understand how the Holy Spirit continues His ministry to us after regeneration
2. To understand how the Holy Spirit takes the place of Jesus in the life of the believer by teaching us, being our advocate, and serving as a divine homemaker

QUOTATION

But when the Helper comes, whom I will send to you from the Father, the Spirit of truth, who proceeds from the Father, he will bear witness about me. And you also will bear witness, because you have been with me from the beginning.

—John 15:26–27

LECTURE OUTLINE

The Work of the Spirit in the Life of the Believer

    A. John 14:16: Jesus promised to send another helper, the *Parakletos*.

        i. *Parakletos* means "to call alongside."

       ii. The Holy Spirit ministers alongside of believers.

B. Jesus states that the Holy Spirit is another help of the same kind as Himself.
    i.   The disciples worried over losing Jesus.
    ii. Jesus reassured them that the Spirit, the other helper, was like Himself.
C. The Spirit demonstrates that He is of the same kind as Jesus because He teaches.
    i.   The disciples had enjoyed three years of Jesus' masterful teaching.
    ii. Jesus promises that the Spirit will teach the marvelous things of God to the hearts of His people, not the least of which will be further revelation concerning the interrelations of the persons of the Trinity.
    iii. The teaching will inspire heightened worship of the Lord.
D. Jesus promises that the Spirit will bear witness to Jesus and reveal to them the things to come.
    i.   The Spirit will remind the disciples of all that Jesus did and reveal to them all the things to come: the content of the New Testament.
    ii. The Holy Spirit will teach the disciples and generations of Christians to come through the revelation of the New Testament.
    iii. Furthermore, the Spirit will illuminate understanding in the heart.
E. Jesus promises to send the Spirit in order that He might counsel His people.
    i.   By counsel, Jesus means that the Spirit will bear witness about Him.
    ii. The Holy Spirit will also bear witness about Jesus through the disciples to the world.
    iii. The Holy Spirit will play the role of both the prosecutor and the defense attorney: He will convict the world and lead them to faith through the disciples, and He will defend them and bear witness to the truth of Christ in them.
F. Jesus promises that the Holy Spirit will be a divine homemaker.
    i.   The Spirit will prepare the hearts of His people for indwelling of the Father and the Son.
    ii. The Spirit, as the homemaker, will transform the heart of the believer so that God might dwell there eternally.

STUDY QUESTIONS

1. The Apostle John is the person most interested in the work of the Holy Spirit.
    a. True
    b. False

2. *Parakletos* means _____ .
    a. "to call from above"
    b. "to call alongside"
    c. "to stir to life"
    d. "to stir into motion"

3. The Spirit will never teach Christians anything more than Jesus taught His disciples.
    a. True
    b. False

4. The *parakletos,* according to the Greek usage of the word, may mean
    _____ .
    a. warrior
    b. friend
    c. advocate
    d. king

5. The Holy Spirit's role as the divine homemaker is the most minor function He serves in the life of a Christian.
    a. True
    b. False

BIBLE STUDY AND DISCUSSION QUESTIONS

1. Why is the Holy Spirit called the *Parakletos*? What does this tell us about the nature of His ministry to believers?

2. How is the Holy Spirit of the same kind as Jesus? How and what does Jesus promise the Spirit will teach His people? Where does Jesus say we learn the teaching of the Holy Spirit?

3. How does the Holy Spirit serve as Jesus' and our counselor?

4. How is the Holy Spirit a divine homemaker?

5. Take some time and reflect on the fact that Jesus loves His people so much He would send His Spirit to perform all the roles Dr. Ferguson discussed in this lesson. What does this reveal about the character of Jesus? The character of the Holy Spirit?

10

Walking in the Spirit

MESSAGE INTRODUCTION

Scripture gives many titles to the Spirit, both explicitly and implicitly. He is our comforter, advocate, and the one who regenerates our hearts and pours life into dust. Yet, there is one title that we pass over simply because of its familiarity: the Spirit is the Holy Spirit. He is holy in and of Himself, and Jesus sends His Holy Spirit to dwell in us in order that we might be holy. Long ago, the Lord commanded "be holy, for I am holy." The Spirit of Jesus aids believers in their sanctification and their growth in the image of our holy Savior.

SCRIPTURE READINGS

Isaiah 6:1–7; Romans 3:21–31; 6:1–11; 7:14–25; 8:1–4, 9–14; 1 Corinthians 6:15; 2 Corinthians 13:14; Galatians 5:16–24; Ephesians 4:30; Philippians 2:12–13

LEARNING OBJECTIVES

1. To understand the importance of some of the titles that the Holy Spirit gives Himself in Scripture
2. To comprehend how the Spirit of God is given to us in order to create holiness
3. To see how the Spirit creates in us motives and desires to live righteous lives for Christ, with whom we are united by the Spirit

QUOTATION

So then, brothers, we are debtors, not to the flesh, to live according to the flesh. For if you live according to the flesh you will die, but if by the Spirit you put to death the deeds of the body, you will live. For all who are led by the Spirit of God are sons of God.

—Romans 8:12-14

LECTURE OUTLINE

I. Titles of the Spirit

    A. Throughout the Bible, titles are given to express the work, purpose, and function of the individuals to which they are ascribed.

    B. The Spirit receives or merits various titles in Scripture.

        i. He is a creator and a re-creator Spirit.

        ii. Jesus refers to the Spirit as the divine Paraclete.

        iii. The Spirit is the Holy Spirit, because He is in Himself holy.

II. The Role of the Holy Spirit in Creating Holiness in the Lives of Believers

    A. The Christian life is filled with a tension between holiness and sin (Rom. 7:14–25).

        i. Christians still possess sin despite their regeneration.

        ii. Yet, as sons and daughters of God, we have a union with Jesus and the indwelling of the Spirit, which demands holiness.

    B. Paul teaches in his letter to the Romans how Christians are able to put to death the deeds of the body through the Spirit.

        i. The Spirit creates in believers a sense that they must put sin to death in their lives (Rom. 6:1–11).

        ii. The Spirit makes the mortification of sin possible.

        iii. The Spirit creates a sense in the believer that he or she is responsible for resisting the temptation to sin (Phil. 2:12–13).

        iv. The Holy Spirit creates in us a desire to be like Christ.

    C. Paul also stresses that the Holy Spirit creates motives in us that make us want to live in a holy fashion (Rom. 8:1–4, 9–14).

        i. The Holy Spirit shifts our attention from the short term to eternity, from the visible to the invisible.

        ii. The Spirit points our eyes on the sacrifice of Jesus Christ, which makes sinning unthinkable.

        iii. The Spirit gives us discernment and a sense of how we should behave.

        iv. The Spirit illuminates our union with Jesus Christ, which makes any form of sinning or being joined to sin unfathomable. This reality demonstrates that when we sin, our sinless, Holy Savior is joined to uncleanness on account of our actions (1 Cor. 6:15).

STUDY QUESTIONS

    1. *Veni Crestor, Spiritus* means _____ .

        a. "Come Holy Spirit"

        b. "Come, Holy Spirit, the Created"

        c. "Come, Holy Spirit, Creator"

        d. "Come, Holy Spirit, with Fire"

2. The Holy Spirit eradicates all sin in the heart of the believer at regeneration.
    a. True
    b. False

3. It is possible, through the Spirit, to keep saying no to sin.
    a. True
    b. False

4. The Spirit gives Christians a general discernment and sense of the place of things in the Christian life.
    a. True
    b. False

5. The Spirit has united us to Jesus for _____ .
    a. short, sporadic intervals of time
    b. the time until His second coming
    c. all eternity
    d. the time until the death of our mortal flesh

BIBLE STUDY AND DISCUSSION QUESTIONS

1. What do we mean when say that the Spirit is the Holy Spirit? What impact does that have on us as Christians?

2. What does it mean to be sons of God (Romans 8:12–13)? How does this affect Christian conduct?

3. What are the four things, according to Dr. Ferguson's analysis of Paul's instruction to the Romans, that the Spirit creates in believers to help them put sin to death in their lives?

4. How does the Spirit create motives within us that make us want to live righteously and in a holy fashion?

5. Since the Holy Spirit unites us to Christ, what implications does this have for Christian living? How does Paul explore this idea in 1 Corinthians 6:15?

11

The Inward Groan

MESSAGE INTRODUCTION

All Christians face the tension in their lives between the promise of complete, permanent restoration and the present state of struggle with sin. Yet, it is important to remember that if we were left alone and unaided, then there would be no struggle on our part, only failure. By the grace of God, the Holy Spirit works on our behalf to transform us into the image of Christ and to assist us in our moral weaknesses. Furthermore, He does not pop in and out at sporadic intervals, exerting only the barest amount of power. On the contrary, just as the Spirit dwells in Jesus, He dwells in us permanently, and He is content to bear the brunt of our burden.

SCRIPTURE READING

Romans 8:1–39

LEARNING OBJECTIVES

1. To understand the task of the Holy Spirit to conform us to the image of Christ, as well as His passion for it
2. To recognize how the Holy Spirit assists us in our moral weaknesses
3. To understand the gracious work of the Trinity, particularly the person of the Spirit, in prayer

QUOTATION

Imagine yourself as a living house. God comes in to rebuild that house. At first, perhaps, you can understand what He is doing. He is getting the drains right and stopping the leaks in the roof and so on; you knew that those jobs needed doing and so you are not surprised. But presently He starts knocking the house about in a way that hurts abominably and does not seem to make any sense. What on earth is He up to? The explanation is that He is building quite a different house from the one you thought of - throwing out a new wing here, putting on an extra floor there, running up towers, making courtyards. You thought you were being made into a decent little cottage: but He is building a palace. He intends to come and live in it Himself.

—C.S. Lewis

LECTURE OUTLINE

The Work of the Holy Spirit in a Christian's Transformation

    A. The Holy Spirit has a passion to make God's people more like Jesus.

    B. Romans 8 provides information concerning how the Holy Spirit assists in this transformation.

        i. Paul frequently employs the term "groaning" in Romans 8.

            1. The earth, Christians, and the Spirit groan.

            2. The groaning does not result from a lack of the Holy Spirit, but it occurs because of His presence.

                a. As Christians, there is a constant tension between present sin and the hope of holiness.

                b. The groaning we experience results from a longing for the day when we will be like Christ. It is not a groan of despair.

        ii. Paul explains that God makes provisions to help us in our moral weakness.

            1. The word for help in 8:26 is *sunantilambanomai*.

                a. The word is prefixed with two seemingly opposite prepositions.

                b. The word means to come along side and assist, normally in a task too great for one party.

            2. The Spirit assists the believer by enabling him to live for the glory of God, a task a Christian cannot perform without the power of the Holy Spirit.

       iii. The Spirit assists in our prayers.

            1. Verse 28 explains that sometimes Christians do not know what to pray for as we ought.

            2. When the Father sees this weakness, He does not take over and remove us from the equation of prayer, but He gives the Spirit.

                a. The Father gives the Spirit, who makes intercession with groans/longings too deep for words.

                b. Because the Spirit knows the mind of the Lord, who reads our hearts, the Spirit enables us to pray according to the perfect will of God in our hearts.

    C. God's willingness to assist in the transformation and weaknesses of His people demonstrates a love and tenderness that merits the utmost gratitude.

STUDY QUESTIONS

1. Paul's driving goal behind the content of Romans 8 is to demonstrate how the Holy Spirit _____ .
   a. is united to Jesus
   b. gives glory to the Father and the Son
   c. overcomes the Devil
   d. conforms believers to the image of Christ

2. If you take the proper steps to experiencing the full power of the Holy Spirit, you will no longer struggle and groan as described in Romans 8.
   a. True
   b. False

3. The word *sunantilambanomai* means _____ .
   a. "to come to the assistance of"
   b. "to take over"
   c. "to thwart"
   d. "to offer minimal help"

4. The Spirit never intercedes on the behalf of believers, for this is the work of the Son only.
   a. True
   b. False

5. A true Christian matures to the state where they always know exactly what to pray for and how to pray for it.
   a. True
   b. False

BIBLE STUDY AND DISCUSSION QUESTIONS

1. Paul uses the language of "groaning" frequently in Romans 8. What is the nature of this groaning and why are Christians doing it?

2. How does the Holy Spirit help us in our moral weakness? How does Paul describe the activity of the Spirit in this process?

3. How does the Spirit help us in our prayers?

4. How does the relationship of the Father to the Spirit assist us in our prayers?

5. Take some time and contemplate the work of the persons of the Trinity in Christian prayer. What does this demonstrate about our God? How will this knowledge alter the way you pray?

12

The Spirit of Sonship

MESSAGE INTRODUCTION

Children need their parents. Yet, at certain times, this need is heightened. The majority of these cases involve distress and suffering. When Paul speaks about the sons of God crying out to their Father, he has these times in mind. Even in times of deepest sorrow, in stages of greatest need, the child of God may cry out to Him with confidence that He desires their supplication. The sons of God have this privileged access on account of the work of the Holy Spirit, who brings us from the darkness into the light of God's family and conforms us to the image of our perfect elder brother, Jesus.

SCRIPTURE READINGS

Luke 11:13; Romans 8; Galatians 4:1–7

LEARNING OBJECTIVES

1. To recognize how the Spirit bears witness with our spirits that we are the children of God
2. To understand the inheritance Christians receive as the sons of God
3. To comprehend the access we have to our caring Father in times of pain and suffering
4. To realize the ultimate goal of the work of the Spirit

QUOTATION

For you did not receive the spirit of slavery to fall back into fear, but you have received the Spirit of adoption as sons, by whom we cry, "Abba! Father!"

—Romans 8:15

LECTURE OUTLINE

I.   The Spirit of Adoption

   A. Romans 8 explains that the work of the Spirit aims at bringing Christians into the
family of God.
      i.   There is no condemnation for those who are in Christ, and they can
never be separated from Him.
      ii. The Spirit of God who comes through Jesus Christ unveils the face of
the Father so that we might, like Jesus, call Him our heavenly Father.
   B. Paul uses the language of sonship in Romans 8 (and Galatians 4) to demonstrate
that all of God's children, male and female alike, receive Jesus' inheritance.
      i.   In Biblical times, daughters did not inherit. Therefore, Paul wants to
make it clear that all of God's children inherit.
      ii. The sons of God, furthermore, are heirs to the full inheritance of Christ,
not just a pittance.
   C. Paul explains that Christians can cry boldly to their Father by virtue of the sonship
purchased by Jesus.
      i.   The Greek word Paul uses for "cry" (*krazo*) refers to a sharp cry of pain.
         1.   All Christians can call out to God in their distress.
         2.   The Father makes Himself accessible in all levels and stages of crisis,
and He delights to receive us as His children.
      ii. This is a great privilege that we as Christians sometimes take for
granted.

II. The Goal of Sonship

   A. The ultimate goal of sonship is to bring glory to the Lord Jesus Christ.
      i.   We cannot define the good Paul speaks about in Romans 8:28 as good
things happening to us.
      ii. The good Paul refers to is our conformity to the image of Christ.
   B. Our conformity to the image of Christ glorifies our Savior because it places Him as
the Savior and firstborn among many brethren.
      i.   We are nothing like our elder brother, Jesus, but the love that the Holy
Spirit has for Jesus has determined that He make us like Him, so that
Jesus might be the firstborn among many brethren.
      ii. The Spirit loves the Father so much that He regenerates sinners to form
a family. The Spirit loves Jesus so much that He makes these sinners
like their elder brother.
   C. Let us praise the Holy Spirit and thank God for His gift.

STUDY QUESTIONS

1. Romans 8 may be summarized in two statements: there is no condemnation for those who are in Christ Jesus, and _____ .
   a. the Spirit intercedes for God's people
   b. God has predestined some for salvation
   c. Jesus now sits at the right hand of the Father
   d. there is nor separation for those who are in Christ Jesus

2. One of the purposes of the Spirit's ministry is to bring us into the family of God.
   a. True
   b. False

3. The sons of God only receive a small portion of the blessings stored up for Jesus Christ.
   a. True
   b. False

4. The Greek word *krazo* refers to a_____.
   a. soft cry
   b. cry of pain
   c. cry of joy
   d. shout of triumph

5. The ultimate goal of the work of the Spirit is to bring glory to Jesus Christ.
   a. True
   b. False

BIBLE STUDY AND DISCUSSION QUESTIONS

1. Why does John Calvin say that the first title of the Holy Spirit is the Spirit of sonship?

2. Why is the New Testament full of Christians speaking to God as their "Heavenly Father"?

3. Why does Paul use the language of "sons of God" when referring to male and female Christians alike in Romans 8? What inheritance do the sons of God receive? How do they receive it?

4. What type of cry does Paul refer to in Romans 8:15? What does this reveal about the plight of the Christian? What does this disclose about the nature of God?

5. What is God's ultimate goal, the purpose of the work of the Holy Spirit? How does God accomplish this? What place do Christians have in this goal?